Sauve Qui Peut

by Lawrence Durrell

*

NOVELS
Monsieur of The Prince of Darkness
The Alexandria Quartet:
Justine, Balthazar, Mountolive, Clea
Justine
Balthazar
Mountolive
Clea
The Revolt of Aphrodite: Tunc, Nunquam
Tunc
Nunquam
The Dark Labyrinth
The Black Book
Livia

LETTERS AND ESSAYS
Spirit of Place edited by Alan G. Thomas

TRAVEL
Bitter Lemons
Reflections on a Marine Venus
Prospero's Cell
Sicilian Carousel
The Greek Islands

POETRY
Vega
The Ikons: and other poems
Selected Poems (new edition)
The Tree of Idleness

DRAMA
Sappho

HUMOUR
Sauve Qui Peut
Stiff Upper Lip
Esprit de Corps
The Best of Antrobus

FOR YOUNG PEOPLE
White Eagles Over Serbia

SAUVE QUI PEUT

by
Lawrence Durrell

Nicolas Bentley drew the pictures

FABER AND FABER
London · Boston

First published in 1966
by Faber and Faber Limited
3 Queen Square London WC1
First published in this edition 1969
Reprinted 1972 and 1979
Printed in Great Britain by
Whitstable Litho Ltd Whitstable Kent
All rights reserved
ISBN 0 571 09224 1

Acknowledgements
to the Editors of:
Playboy and *Weekend Telegraph* for *Sauve Qui Peut*
Mademoiselle for *What-Ho on the Rialto!*
Mademoiselle and *Harper's Bazaar* for *High Barbary*
Saturday Evening Post and *Town* for *The Little Affair in
Paris*. *Playboy* for *All to Scale*
Playboy and *Weekend Telegraph* for *A Corking Evening*
Argosy for *Aunt Norah*

Contents

Sauve Qui Peut

We dips (said Antrobus) are brought up to be resourceful, to play almost any part in life, to be equal to any emergency almost—how else could one face all those foreigners? But the only thing for which we are not prepared, old man, is blood.

Blood?

Blood!

Mind you, I am thinking of exceptional cases, out-of-the-way incidents; but they are not as rare as one might imagine. Old Gulliver, for example, was invited to an execution in Saigon to which he felt it was his duty to go. It affected him permanently, it damaged his concentration. His head is quite over on one side, he twitches, his ears move about. Unlucky man! I cannot claim an experience as radical as his, but I can speak of one which was almost as bad. Imagine, one fine day we are delivered a perfectly straightforward invitation card on which we read (with ever-widening eyes) the following text or something like it:

9

SAUVE QUI PEUT

> *His Excellency Hacsmit Bey and Madame Hacsmit Bey joyfully invite you to the Joyful Circumcision of their son Hacsmit Hacsmit Abdul Hacsmit Bey. Morning dress and decorations. Refreshments will be served.*

You can imagine the long slow wail that went up in the Chancery when first this intelligence was brought home to us. Circumcision! Joyfully! Refreshments! "By God, here is a strange lozenge-shaped affair!" cried De Mandeville, and he was right.

Of course, the Embassy in question was a young one, the country it represented still in the grip of mere folklore. But still I mean . . . The obvious thing was to plead indisposition, and this we did as one man. But before we could post off our polite, almost Joyful refusals to these amiable Kurds, Polk-Mowbray called a general meeting in Chancery. He was pensive, he was pale and grave, quite the Hamlet. "I suppose you have all received this" he said, holding up a pasteboard square on which the dullest eye could descry the sickle and minarets of the Kurdish Arms with the sort of crossed cruets underneath.

"Yes" we chorused.

"I suppose you have all refused" went on our Chief, "and in a way, I am glad. I don't want my Mission to develop a taste for blood . . . these things grow on one. But it does raise rather a problem, for the Kurds are a young, buoyant, up-and-coming little country with a rapidly declining economy, and they are fearfully touchy. It is inconceivable that HMG should not be represented at this affair by *one* of us. Besides, who knows, it might be informal, touching, colourful, even instructive . . . what the devil? But *someone* should be there; we just can't ignore two-legged Kurds in the modern world. The next thing is they will vote against us in UNO. You take my point?"

"Well, I have sat up all night worrying about the affair, and (having no taste for blood myself) have arrived at a perfectly democratic solution which I know you will approve and I hope you will respect."

From behind his back came his left hand holding a packet of straws.

"Whoever draws the shortest straw will represent us" he cried shrilly. We all paled to the gums but what could we do? It was a command. Closing our eyes, lips moving in prayer, we drew. Well and . . . yes, of course I did. I drew that short straw.

I let out—I could not help it—a rueful exclamation, almost a shout. "But surely, Sir . . ." I cried. But Polk-Mowbray, his face full of compassion, smote me on the shoulder. "Antrobus" he said, "I could not have wished for anyone more reliable, more circumspect, more jolly unflinching, anyone less likely to faint. I am glad—yes, glad with all my heart that fate should have chosen you. *Courage, mon vieux.*"

This was all very well. I wasn't a bit cockered up by all this praise. My lip trembled, voice faltered. "Is there no other way?" I cried out in my anguish, gazing from face to stony face. There wasn't it would seem. Polk-Mowbray shook his head with a kind of sweet sadness, like a Mother Superior demobbing a novice. "It is *kismet*, Antrobus" he said and I felt a sort of coffin-lid close on me. I squared my shoulders and let my chin fall with a thump onto my chest. I was a beaten man. I thought of my old widowed mother in St Abdomen in the Wold—what would she say if she knew? I thought of many things. "Well" I said at last. "So be it." I must say, everyone brightened up, looked awfully relieved. Moreover, for the next few days I received every mark of consideration from my colleagues. They spoke to me in Hushed Voices, Hushed Commiserating Voices, as if I were an invalid; they tiptoed about for fear of disturbing my reveries. I thought of a hundred ways out of the affair but none of them seemed practicable. I went so far as to sit in a draught hoping I would catch pneumonia; I hinted broadly that I would surrender my stalls for the Bolshoi to anyone kind enough to replace me —in vain.

At last the day dawned; there was nothing for it but to climb into sponge-bag and hoist gongs. At last I was ready. The whole Chancery was lined up to shake my hand and see me off. Polk-Mowbray had put the Rolls at my disposal, pennant and all. "I've told the driver to take a First-Aid Kit with him" he said hoarsely. "One never knows in these matters." You would have thought that *I* was to be the sacrificial lamb from the way he went on. De Mandeville pressed his smelling-salts into my hand and said brokenly "Do give little Abdul all our sympathy." As for Dovebasket, he pressed his Leica upon me saying "Try and get a close-up. The Sunday Times colour sup is crying out for something new and they pay like fiends—I'll split with you. It's one chance in a million to scoop Tony." The little blackhead! But I was too broken to speak. I handed the thing back without a word and stepping into the car cried faintly "To the Kurdish Embassy, Tobias."

The Kurds had everything arranged most tastefully, I must say; lots of jolly decent-looking refreshments laid out in a huge marquee on the back lawn. Here we dips congregated. I noticed that most Missions had sent acting

vice-consuls smelling for the most part of brandy and
looking pale and strained. Now the Kurds may be a young
nation but they look as crafty as some of the older. The
Mission was dressed in spanking *tenue* but in one corner,
presiding over a side-table covered in grisly-looking
Stone Age instruments, stood a small group of sinister
men clad in horse-blankets of various colours. They had
shaven skulls and purple gums and they conversed in a
series of dry clicks like Bushmen. Faces which suggested
nothing so much as open-cast coal-mining. This, I took
it, was the Medical Wing of the Kurdish Embassy—the
executioners. But where was the little beardless youth in
whose honour all this joyful frolic had been arranged? I
went so far as to ask.

"Ah" cried the Ambassador, "he will be here in a
minute. He is on his way from the airport. He arrived
from London this afternoon." I was a bit puzzled by this,
but . . . Kurds have their own way of doing things. "And
think of it!" went on the Head of Mission, clasping his
hands. "Abdul knows nothing of all this. It is a surprise
for him, a little surprise. He will be very joyful when he
sees. . . ." He waved at the group of executioners. Well, I
thought to myself, let joy be unconfined, and tried to
draw strength from some rather good *rahat lokoum*—
Turkish Delight—which I found in a corner. After all,
one could close one's eyes, or turn the head; one needn't
actually *look*, I told myself.

Luckily my fears were groundless. Imagine our collective surprise when Abdul bounded into the tent to
embrace his mother and father: instead of some puling
adolescent, we beheld a tough-looking youth of some
twenty summers with a handsome moustache and a frank
open countenance. This was to be the victim! I must say,

his frank open countenance clouded as he took in the import of the business. He showed every sort of unwillingness to enter into the full joyfulness of the occasion. Wouldn't you? Moreover, he was just down from Oxford where he had not only taken a good degree, but had got his boxing blue. His mother and father looked troubled and began to urge, to plead, in Kurdish.

But he respectfully declined, giving every mark of disapprobation. He shook his head violently and his eye flashed. At last his father lost patience and motioned to the thugs in the corner. He was going to force him to enter into the joyfulness of the occasion. But the young man had learned something at Oxford. With a right and left he sent two sprawling; the others climbed on his back. A terrible fracas broke out. Cartwheeling round like a top with the Kurds on his back, Abdul mowed half the Corps down and upset the trestle tables; then, reversing, knocked the tent-pole out and the whole thing collapsed on us in a billowing cloud of coloured stuff. Shouts, yells ... I lost my topper, but managed to crawl out from under. I tottered to the gate yelling for Tobias. All I got out of the affair was the box of Turkish Delight which I shared round the Chancery. It met with approval and I was the hero of the hour. Compliments? They fairly forked them up to me. Polk-Mowbray was in two minds about the sort of figure I had cut, but after giving it thought he summed the matter up jolly sagely. "In diplomacy" he said, "it is so often a case of *sauve qui peut.*"

What-ho on the Rialto!

In the Old Days (said Antrobus) before Time Was—I think it was the year that Mrs Gaskell won the Nobel for England—diplomacy was a quiet and restful trade carried on in soothing inanity among a hundred shady legations and embassies all over the globe. It was hardly more taxing than Divinity for a Scotchman. A fond bland light shone from the old dip's eyes——and why not? Minted at Eton, moulded by Balliol, and mellowed to the sunset tone of old brick by a Grand Tour, the fellow was in clover and he knew it. Handpicked, packaged, dusted over lightly with male hormone, he was delivered to his post without a bally scratch. Then he had pride: he shaved with nothing but Yardley and scented his beard with Imperial Saddle. Look at the change now: fellows dashed over with cheap and perhaps combustible shaving lotions and industrial talc. Moreover, something else has happened; how has your modern dip acquired his present pinched and furtive look? I will tell you.

It came with The Fall. One day the slumbering dragon

in the heart of Personnel awoke and roared: "Let Woman be given high office." Woman, dear God! It was the end, old man, and we knew it. We paled to the nape. Our ears went back and stayed pressed close to the head. Urgent confabs took place all over the Office on the intercoms. A hundred voices rose in protest, a hundred plans were made to scotch the idea. Some even spoke of assassination for Gavin Pyecraft who had hatched this grisly scheme. He had always been unbalanced (grammar school). A sort of mystic. He liked custard poured over his prunes. But despite all our efforts the idea caught on and spread. The rot set in abroad as well. It travelled like the Spanish 'flu. First vice-consuls (a suitable enough title) then Information Girls and finally Female Ambassadors.

All of which brings me to the particular event with which I hope to illustrate my general contention. The French sent in a woman Ambassador to Vulgaria in the form of a handsome, slightly moustached young widow called Mole with a parlous amount of frou-frou and a deadly languid voice which lifted one slightly in one's shoes. The Mission, of course, reeled under the blow, but what could they do? You could hear throats being cleared as she passed. She Walked in Beauty, old Man, Like the Night, to quote someone who ought to have known; easily, lightly, as if on ball-bearings. It made conference difficult to begin with. She had such a lot of different hats; and the way, just the way, she accepted an Aide-Mémoire from the trembling hand of a Head of Chancery made him burn like a volcano.

All might have gone well—but how *could* it?—had not fate at that moment sent in Bonzo di Porco as Italian Head of Chancery. Bonzo was born to be De Mandeville's

rival. You never met Bonzo, did you? Well, all tech-
nicalities aside, and absolutely without prejudice, he was
a fitful little *numero* indeed. He claimed to be several types
of prince and count; his underclothes were spattered with
crowns; he drove a cream Hispano-Suiza twice the size
of De Mandeville's Rolls. *His* chauffeur was much larger
too, and dressed like Robin Hood. Well! You can understand De Mandeville feeling put down. Of course, both
men were well-bred in a nervous, mediocre sort of way
and it is possible that the iron laws of the Service might
have prevented an open breech—had it not been for The
Woman.

She flattered Bonzo, making him show off his talents
where someone more intelligent might have persuaded
him to leave them in the napkin. He played, for example,
the flute better, louder, than De Mandeville. His pout was
professional, his puff serene and not wavery like that of his
rival. Apart from this, he played a blazing game of shuttle-
cock. He had actually once had leprosy. . . . Oh, I know.
You could go on about Bonzo's qualities for ever. But
they just made De Mandeville bite his nails down to the
quick and *kick* his chauffeur. At Oxford Bonzo had got a
first in Lampshade Making while poor De M. had to be
content with a mouldy third in Comparative Lipsticks.

The first round opened with a bit of mild vapouring and
vaunting on quite a high intellectual plane—again because
of You Know Who. Where you have French people, you
find culture creeping in. ("Why" she had the nerve to ask
me one day "are you fond of Racine?" to which I riposted
instantly: "I never bet on horses, Madam.")

Well, Bonzo gave it out that he was the only prince in
Christendom with a special dispensation enabling him, if
he wished, to ride a horse into Milan Cathedral. But he

didn't wish, he added modestly. Fifteen—love. Now De Mandeville announced that he had a chit from the A. of C. enabling him to enter the Pump Room in Bath on hands and knees, should he so wish. Fifteen—all. As for the lady, she went on enmeshing them with her veni vidi vici. She had an indelible habit of tapping you on the lips with her closed fan which won all hearts. People queued to be tapped, but none more ardently than Bonzo and his rival. You should have seen them putting up their little faces—like a couple of rudimentary Chinese geese. Their encounters at her table, albeit couched in a highly allusive intellectual vein, were getting more and more acrimonious. De Mandeville started a war of quotations which harassed his enemy on the flank until Dovebasket pinched his "Dictionary of" and sold it to Bonzo privately. De Mandeville said—just as an example—that when Shakespeare wrote the words "more honoured in the breech than the observance" he was thinking of someone like Bonzo. Thirty-forty. Bonzo replied that the poet Wordsworth wrote:

> *"A varlet by the river's brim*
> *A simple varlet was to him"*

when he was clearly thinking of somebody of the De Mandeville Stamp. Deuce.

It could only end one way. One evening, at a cultural soirée in the Froggish Embassy, they came to an open breech as to who should turn over the lady's music. Pull followed pull, push, push. I ask you to believe me when I say there was a mild scuffle. They pulled each other's ties and stamped. The lady fainted, and leaving her like a fallen ninepin, they stormed out into the night in different directions.

WHAT-HO ON THE RIALTO!

At this point De Mandeville said it couldn't go on. De Mandeville said that the world wasn't big enough for him and Bonzo too—one of them would have to go. De Mandeville referred darkly to duelling pistols, but when Dovebasket produced some, he showed a marked disinclination to touch them. Dovebasket worked with all the ferocious power of his evil genius to get these two frantic men up to the popping crease but they wouldn't bat, it seems. Dovebasket sent both of them repeated challenges in each other's names trying to help the situation to mature fruitfully. But no. Somehow they managed . . . but as a matter of fact, I mean, what could one visualize as being suitable weapons for single combat—syringes?

But Dovebasket wasn't finished yet; he had recently seen an Italian opera and had been much struck by the presence throughout the action of some fellows of gamesome look on the stage: they appeared to have no stable employment, to be of no fixed abode, and to be loitering with intent. What they did do, occasionally, was to slit a throat on request for a derisory sum—the price of a second helping. Their clients were all in high places and hoping to inherit from the people whose weazands had been slit by this little band of chaps—these "bravos" for that is the word. Dovebasket was charmed by a profession so . . . how would you put it? It differs slightly from diplomacy, anyway. He persuaded De Mandeville that the bravo was by no means extinct and that Bonzo had several of them suborned in his Embassy. He, De Mandeville, should watch out. He did much the same to Bonzo, and for a while they neither of them dared to go out after dark. From this it was but a step to persuade both men to pay a large sum to a couple of Chancery Guards to be their bodyguards. These they armed to the teeth with an air-pistol. Dovebasket got a percentage. But he was not finished yet.

Came the fateful fancy-dress ball given by the unsuspecting Norwegians: in the Chancery we groaned as we noticed the stipulations about dress: "Masked and about to spend an evening of Carnival in the sixteenth century". Everyone groaned: this meant we should all have to borrow costumes once more from the wardrobe of the National Opera. Venice! De Mandeville knitted harder than ever as he wondered whether perhaps he might not be poled into the Embassy lying down in a gondola in a cloak? He was toying with this idea and explaining its virtues to me—Bonzo would never think up anything like that—when Rosencrantz, I mean Dovebasket, came sidling in to whisper in his ear. What he said parched him a bit. Apparently Bonzo was going to press things to their limit: his bravos had orders to get De Mandeville during the masked ball. "I certainly should not stir without your own bravos" said Dovebasket.

"But it's in costume!"

"Then they too will be costumed and armed. I should see that they have a sword and buckler each at least—if not a reversible bassinet too."

"Why reversible?"

"To catch the blood in."

"I see."

De Mandeville looked somewhat pale. Dovebasket slipped away to telephone to Bonzo in much the same terms and made his flesh creep at the thought that De Mandeville and his two bravos had decided to eliminate him. Which would get who first . . . that was the problem, if you understand me. How?

Well then, let us turn to that fatal evening. You must

22

picture us—a rather listless mob of strangely shaped men clad in brilliant but somewhat grubby reminiscences of Venice. Enormous trousers which our robust forefathers used I think to term "gallygaskins": two hundred bolts of bombazine to every tuck. Then enamelled codpieces with dependent froggings and perhaps a calico fascinator or two. Moreover, we were all masked and wore upon our heads those strange hats which are apparently given away with every free D. Litt at Oxford. Lampshades, old man, snuffers, dreaming abat-jours of Oxenford.

Well, there we all were, after some insipid chamber-music, when the wrath of the Lord was unleashed. Dovebasket suddenly, with no warning, unsheathed a service-able-looking cutlass, gave a fearful growl like a mastiff, and launched a terrific slash at . . . I blush to say it . . . his innocent white-haired old Ambassador. "Answer for your sins, Mowbray" he yelled as he drove the weapon home. Well, not quite home. In matters of self-interest, Polk-Mowbray could show a turn of speed. It was the public interest which rendered him lethargic. He had been having a delicious evening, full of clean fun, and admired his costume which made him feel like the Bashaw of Hendon. Now suddenly this apparent maniac was on him nip and tuck. It is to his credit that his jump took him almost to the mantelpiece. Dovebasket wheeled about and addressed himself to the American Minister, who gave a wail of mortal terror and manfully unsheathed his own sword and fended off the lunatic, being driven swiftly back to the garden balustrade over which he fell into a flowerbed. He had hardly time to ask what in the name of flaming Jesus was going forward before disappearing into the void. Everyone was startled and drew their swords. Some started as a joke, but no sooner were they poked than they turned nasty. The women screamed and got under the piano. Pretty soon a general melee started and I decided that it was time for me to seek the only place of shelter on such evenings—the curtains. It is perhaps the Polonius in me, and I am not unmindful of his fate; nevertheless. . . . By now there was a dreadful noise of cold steel on steel, like some fearful knife-grinders' agape. It is a mercy no one was actually killed. Perhaps the swords were from "property" or perhaps it is just that dip skins are inordinately thick. Anyway, apart from the Chaplain who was transfixed to the grand piano through his gaskins, no harm was done; people began to unmask and the panic to die down. Only, in the centre of the room, six figures still clashed away; I took it that they were Bonzo and De Mandeville with their respective bravos. This looked much more spirited and even promising. Pretty soon, one felt, there would be some figures lying Strangely Still upon the carpet, and one of them, Pray God, would be De Mandeville. But no. Heaven intervened in the shape of the butler, Drage, bible in hand. With his experienced eye he took in the scene; with his experienced hand he did the only thing. He stooped and pulled the carpets and the contestants, reeling, fell—their hats rolling off, their masks slipping. A singular sight was revealed. Bonzo had been fighting his own bravos. So had De Mandeville. It was a miracle that neither had been punctured. While they were still sitting on the floor comes this female Ambassador and in a voice of thunder, I mean the voice of a thrush, shouts, no, I mean warbles: "I order you to desist." She tapped their lips and they were speechless. She ordered them to make it up and with a groan they fell into each other's arms. So ended this fearful ordeal.

Well, from then on things went a bit better and both

men won their service medals; as for the lady, she afterwards went to Russia, they say, taking her culture with her, and there had quite a success. She liked the place, the people, and the system so much that she had herself nationalized and married a collective farm. Presumably there she is today. But in my view, old man, woman's place has always been on the farm.

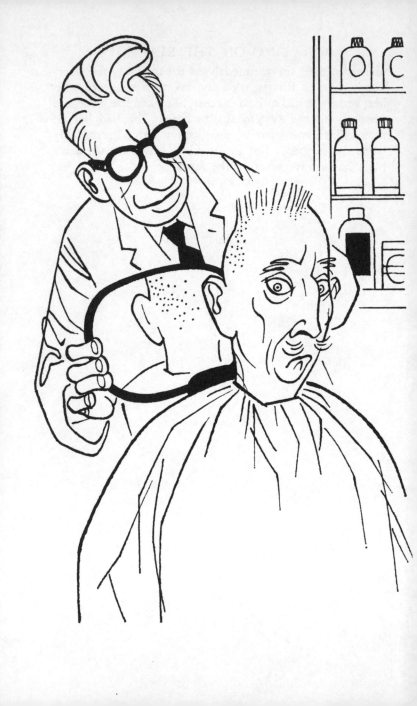

High Barbary

What I very much enjoy on the second Saturday of the month (said Antrobus) is the little walk across to the Strand for a haircut and a spiritual revamping *chez* the good Fenner. Everything about the operation is reassuring, soothing. As you know, Fenner himself is clearly a mixture of Old Father Time and Dr Freud. The whole Office has, at one time or another, passed through his purposeful scissors. You know how fanatically faithful to tradition the FO is; well, Fenner is a tradition. Why, last week when Toby Featherblow's wife, Constance, popped number four and the thing was found to be positively covered in hair, it was to Fenner that they rushed to have the features disinterred for the purposes of licensing and registration. Otherwise the registrar might have refused to accept what was, to all intents and purposes, an ape. Yes, you can count on old Fenner. He never flinches before reality.

As for the Emporium—with its potted palms, painted mirrors, its pictures of Eights Week in the 'nineties, its dominating portrait of Gladstone staring out through (or perhaps round?) a Fenner hairdo—what is one to say? It radiates calm and the soothing smell of bay rum or Fenner's Scalp Syrup and Follicle Food combined. Nor does one overhear any low conversation there—just a few choice anecdotes about the Dutch Royal Family, carefully phrased. Fenner is strict: once I remember that two military attachés were expelled from their stools for trying to exchange betting slips. Fenner's scorn was so withering that one of them cried.

But all this one learns to value truly only when one has served abroad—for not the least of the hazards the poor dip has to face is that of foreign barbary. My dear chap, as you walk in, you can scan the row of seated clients and tell at a glance where some of them have been serving. The singular bottlebrush effect of a Siamese haircut, for example, will take ages to grow out and is quite unmistakeable. Fenner will shake his head commiseratingly and say, "Bangkok, I take it, sir?" The poor chap will sit with trembling lip and nod sadly. "We will see what can be done to save you, sir" says Fenner and releases a faintly flocculent blast from a pressurized syringe, which at once brings back the flush of health to the raped scalp. You have experienced it. You will know what I mean.

It varies, too, with every country, as do the habits of the various artists. In Italy your barber is apt to sing—a dangerous habit and excruciating for the tone-deaf; moreover he may add gestures to his little aria of a sudden and lop off an earlobe with a fine air of effortless self-distinction. Personally, I would rather have the stuff grow all the way down my back and into my chair than trust an Italian when overcome with emotion and garlic. I have seen it happen. A cousin of Polk-Mowbray still bears a cropped right ear; indeed, he is lucky to have as much of it left as he has—only a wild swerve prevented its total disappearance. Talk about living dangerously!

In places like Germany, for example, one is lucky to be able to get away without a severed carotid. As for the Balkans, they, too, have their fearsome methods, and I have known cases where people took to beards and shingles rather than face up to reality. Of course, the moment they get leave they fly back to Fenner, who cuts back all the undergrowth and serenely removes whatever may have been picked up by the static electricty. At least that was the excuse that Munnings-Mather gave for all the hairpins and Gramophone needles Fenner found in *his* beard.

As for the French—they leave me speechless, positively beating the air. They will either do you a *style pompier*, piling the muck up on the top of your head and pressure-greasing it until you leave marks on the ceiling of every lift you enter, or else they treat you to a razor cut of such topiary ferocity that you come out feeling sculpted. They cut into the stuff as if it were cheese. No. No. You can have Paris. Let me keep my modest tonsure and my Short-Back-and-Sides Outlook. The Style Fenner (vintage 1904) is my sort of thing.

Why, in Vulgaria, once, things got so bad that Polk-Mowbray was driven, positively driven, to Take Steps—and you know how much he hated the naked thrust of Action. It was during the Civil War when the country was Communist all the week and Royalist at the weekends. Every Saturday morning the Royalist troops came down from the hills and took the Praesidium; every Monday morning they were driven back with heavy losses. Monday was payday for the Communist forces, Saturday that of the Royalist army. This had a strange effect on the hairdressing business, for during the week you only found heavily nationalized barbers at work, while at the weekend you could borrow the five Royal barbers from the other side. The Communists used an unpretentious pudding-basin cut which had been worked out in terms of the dialectic, lightly driving a harrow across the scalp and then weeding with finger and thumb. They were short of instruments because the Five-Year Plan hadn't started to work due to lack of foreign capital. Anyway, during the week you were in the hands of some horny peasant, while if you waited till Sunday you could get a sort of Viennese pomadour which fanned away into wings at the back like a tail coat and carried sideburns of a corkscrew pattern which once made Polk-Mowbray look so like Elizabeth Barrett Browning that the British Council man, Gool, suggested . . . but that is another story.

Yes, the Balkan barber, conditioned by the hirsute nature of his client, has developed a truly distressing style of action—suited to the nature of the *terrain*, I don't doubt, but nonetheless frightful to those who have been decently brought up. They positively plunge into one's nostrils, hacking and snipping as if they were clearing a path in the jungle; then before one can say "moustache cup" they crawl into one's ears, remorselessly pruning at what (to judge by the sound) must be something as intractable as a forest of holm oak. I shall spare you. You know.

But I think you had left before Polk-Mowbray entered his Do-It-Yourself phase; the state of Vulgarian barbary must have touched him off. He saw an advertisement for an instrument called, I think, The Gents Super Hair Regulator, which from the brochure appeared to be an ingenious comb and razor blade in one; you trimmed as you combed, so to speak. Nothing simpler, nothing more calculated to please. Polk-Mowbray, deeply moved by the discovery, ordered a dozen, one for each member of the Chancery. He was beside himself with pride and joy. Speaking from a full heart, he said: "From today our troubles are over. I want each one of you from now on to use his little Regulator and so boycott these heathen barbers of Vulgaria." Well, I don't know if you know the Regulator? No? Be warned then. It is not a toy for frolicking amateurs. The keenest professional skill is needed to work it. Otherwise, it takes huge lumps out of your hair in the most awkward places, leaving gaunt patches of white scalp glimmering through. By lunchtime on that fatal day, the whole Chancery looked as if it had been mowed down by ringworm or mange. Worse still, De Mandeville contracted a sort of scalp-rot which turned his whole skull green. A sort of deathly verdigris set in. He had to keep his hair in a green baize bag for over a week while Fenner's Follicle Food did its healing work—lucky I had brought a bottle with me. But, of course, the sight nearly drove Polk-Mowbray berserk, especially as at that time the two were at daggers drawn. De Mandeville had sworn to try and drive his chief mad by a sort of verbal Chinese torture. To every remark made to him, he would only reply "Charmed,—I'm sure," with a kind of snakelike sibilance. It doesn't sound much, but I assure you that after a few days of endless repetition of this phrase (accompanied by the fearful sight of the green baize bag on his head), Polk-Mowbray was practically beaten to his knees.

But probably the most horrifying instance of mass barbary that I recall was what befell the little party of guileless Finns who submitted themselves to a Vulgarian perm in preparation for the National Lepers' Day Ball. That could not be bettered as an illustration of the Things One Is Up Against in the Service. Five of them, including the Ambassadress, were partially electrocuted owing to a faulty fuse. How is it, I ask myself, that they did not know that the light and power arrangements of Vulgaria were so capricious? Yet, they did not. Polk-Mowbray, who was wooing the Communists, had given the Minister for Interior an electric razor which, whenever it was plugged in, fused the lights of the capital. Something of this order must have happened to the innocent Finns. With their crowning glories tied into those sort of pressurized domes attached to the ceiling by a live wire, they were suddenly aware that everything was turning red-hot and beginning to smoke fearfully; the atmosphere was rapidly beginning to resemble that of a Turkish bath that has got out of control. But the Finns are normally an unemotional race and not much given to fruitless ratiocination. It was not until sparks an inch long began to sprout from their fingers that they began to wonder dimly if all was well. By then it was too late.

They were far too hot to hold. The barbers who manfully tried to disengage them retired hastily with burns and shock. In fact they might have been there to this day, fried to a crisp, had not the Diplomatic Corps been passing at that moment in full *tenue*. We were winding our way across the town to lay a rather limp wreath on the Leper Memorial when we saw the smoke and heard the shrill ululations of the feckless barbers. It was more than lucky, too, that Dovebasket should have a pair of rubberized pliers in his uniform pocket. He darted into the smoke-filled cavern and brought his mechanical genius to bear on the situation, snipping the live wires which attached

our poor colleagues to the roof. The Finns rolled moaning
to the floor in their golden domes, looking like so much
science fiction. "Give them air" we all cried shrilly, and
willing hands carried them out and laid them in a row
upon the pavements. All this had the superficial air of
being a mass burial, and I personally believe that had it
been anyone but the Finns, that would indeed have been
the case. But the Finns can take anything with equani-
mity. Water was carefully poured over them from plastic
buckets. They smoked, they smelled like chops frying,
but at last they came to their senses.

We did not see them again until the ball that night which
closed Leper Week. My dear chap, you have never im-
agined such hair. It was positively psychoanalytic. Golden
wigs of such hellish, blinding, metallic brilliance. The
demon barbers had certainly done their work. . . . Ah!
But I see that Fenner is free at last. More of this anon.

Seraglios and Imbroglios

If you were to surmise (said Antrobus) that all our problems in the Vulgarian Mission were political ones you would be Gravely In Error. The dip's life is never as clear cut as the Wars of the Roses; in fact its sheer variety is equalled only by its inanity—as Poincaré once nearly said. Perhaps that is why we enjoy such a range of topics for conversation—no facet of experience has left us unmarked. That is why your hardened dip is not the man to be unnerved merely by the patter of rain on a brushed bowler. He has seen deeply into the secrets of nature. Well, my boy, these reflections—graver than is my wont —have been pooped off by today's *Times* which announces that old Sammy is finishing his memoirs. Poor old Sam—he was once described admiringly by Eisenhower as a supramundane lush. I expect he is going to get his own back in print somehow; he can just read and write—Eton, of course. But it's slow work and it must have taken him years to amount to a book. And then, of course, he's getting on and his career was often dappled with shadow. I mean, he started out with a regulation hip-flask and ended by drinking unrefined embrocation from a hip-bath. Or so they say in the Bag Room where the actual hip-bath may still be viewed for a small *douceur*. No-one was really surprised when he took refuge in the Church. For years now we've had vague reports of him stumping round some sodden Suffolk parish clad in a strip of roofing felt. At Xmas time . . . but why go on? The man has suffered; he is trying to atone by a little mild beadling. In the long unheated nights he sits and writes. What does he write? Well may you ask what old Sam is writing. It is not *The Schoolgirls' Wonderbook of Booze and Sex*—no. It is a volume of DIPLOMATIC MEMOIRS. Its title is *Seraglios and Imbroglios* or *Glimpses Behind the Bead Curtain of Diplomacy by One Who Was There and Suffered For It*. Has a sinister sort of ring, no? God knows I hope—everyone hopes—he will be discreet.

My misgivings have increased of late after a talk to Gormley who claims to have spoken to Sam recently on the phone. Apparently Sam said it was all about diplomacy from the religious angle. Now that puzzled me. The only religious chap we had was the chaplain and he left under a cloud, all hushed up. And yet . . . I wonder. There were strange aspects of our lives out there which I suppose one could call religious—if one strained the Official Secrets Act until it creaked. Morris-dancing on the lawn—wouldn't that qualify? With De Mandeville and his chauffeur all cross-gartered and with gipsy earrings. But there was nothing religious about Polk-Mowbray's outburst when he saw them. . . .

Then I remember little Carter—if that was the name. Americans are notoriously Romance Prone. He went off to Egypt on leave with the ALEXANDRIA QUARTET under his arm. Next thing we knew, he had become a Moslem —bang! just like that. Gone over to them bodily. He came back from leave looking pale but jaunty in a ghastly sort of way and towing a string of little new black wives. Real ones. "Durrell's right" he is alleged to have announced to his Chief with an airy wave. "Down there almost everything goes." Well, of course, he went too; but he had brought us a headache. Things like this can be very catching in the Corps. He had Raised a Precedent. Yet technically he was quite within his rights. There was no religious bar in the State Department nor in the F.O. They had the devil's own job to post him: there was no excuse—being American he was efficient. Nothing left but to upgrade him and send him to UNO where he would be lost in the dusky spectrum. I met Schwartz their Councillor looking pale and fagged out; I knew why. It was this damned business, all the telegrams flying about.

"It was such a quiet mission" he wailed, "before This. What did he want to do it for?" Schwartz played bridge every day of the week and the thing was gumming up his concentration. Through the open window we could see Carter taking his wives for an airing on the Embassy lawn; since they could not speak each other's language, he was playing leap-frog with them. The staff stared down through the windows, their faces working. Schwartz stifled an oath. "Antrobus" he said, "you know and I know that technically speaking there is nothing in the regulations to prevent King Solomon strolling into the State Department and asking for a posting—even if he were to jerk his thumb (here Schwartz jerked his thumb) and say 'These ladies here, by the way, are my wife; kindly put her on K rations.' " I felt for him. Yes, Carter cost us a great deal of extra legislation. After all, what was to prevent the whole State Department filling up one night with Mormons? Well, the waters closed over little Carter. I was sorry for him. Two of the wives were quite pretty, they said, with well-placed Advantages. But it was useless crying over spilt milk. We reformed our ranks and marched on, ever on.

You see what I mean? Hardly the sort of thing one wants written up by Sam. Besides, this Carter episode touched off a powder-barrel in our own Mission. We were unaware that we were sitting on it. Mind you, I had smelled burning for some time but couldn't locate the site. You remember Drage? Of course you do. Yes, here we are truly in the field of Revealed Religion. All that winter the Visions had been gaining on him, the Voices had been whispering seditious info. into his faun-like ears. Also he was at war with Dovebasket—always a dangerous thing, and now doubly so for that human vacuum had just taken a degree in applied electronics. Drage alarmed me, Dovebasket disgusted. I held no brief for either. But things went from Bad to Worse, and the food began to go to blazes. The Instant Pudding refused to stand to attention. Dovebasket had fixed the bunsens in the kitchen to such good purpose that Drage virtually found himself supervising nuclear tests with self-raising flour. De Mandeville worked out a Menu for the French Mission Dinner which was too near the bone to raise anything but the hollowest of laughs. It spoke of plovers' eggs in ether and baby rusks marinated in nitric acid. It hinted at cocktails of lemon curd and ammonia with just a touch of machine oil from the crank-case of some abandoned locomotive. Gods! There was even the British

Club Sandwich which he diagnosed as consisting of old raffia work with thin slices of thrice-triturated gymnosophist. Drage seemed to have gone dead Continental. And still the Visions pressed on him, thicker and faster. Finally Drage was forced to ask for religious help from the leader of his sect—a Nonconformist preacher called Fly-Fornication Wilkinson. He was a tall spindly man with a goatee and huge goggles. Little comfort, I should have thought, could be derived from his strange allure. But what to do? We could all see that the fellow had a mushroom-shaped psyche. His voice was deep and boomy with an occasional scream like a police whistle on the word "sin" which made one sit up and metaphorically spurn the gravel with one's hooves. He moved into Drage's cottage to offer him the occasional winged word. Next thing was Drage asked if he might address us on a Sunday and preach a sermon. The Chaplain was away playing roulette in Nice that week. In matters of religion we are extremely liberal. I could hardly refuse.

The fellow took as his text "King Solomon in all his glory was not arrayed as one of these." The hats of the Embassy ladies had apparently caused him grave offence. He pointed at them as he lashed out at us. His words whistled through the side-chapel like grape-shot. De Mandeville paled and began to sob quietly into a cambric handkerchief. To hear him you would have thought the typists' pool was rotten to the core and that Polk-Mowbray was living a life of untrammelled lubricity with a cageful of nightingales. I must say!

Yet for the first time as we listened we all began to feel a kind of sneaking pride in Dovebasket, a warmth about the heart. He had bugged the pulpit. He was going to avenge us—even though his real target had been the un-

fortunate Drage. Never mind. The Rev. Fly-Fornication
was going to receive the charge. I must say, though, he
was game: despite every set-back he plunged on with his
sermon. Flames leapt from the harmonium when Miss
Todger's elfin foot touched the treadles. They were gal-
lantly beaten out with Polk-Mowbray's overcoat. Wilkinson resumed his discourse. Electronic devices buried in
the walls now opened up a barrage of jungle music, cow-
bells, mating cats and so on. Wilkinson tightened his pegs
and let his voice soar above it. Then on the wall behind
us appeared a giant coloured projection which said
"REPENT YOU DOGS" and then another saying, "DRAGE,
I'VE COME FOR YOU, YOU BASTARD." This was signed
"Jaweh" in an illiterate schoolchild's hand. It was clearly
going to be a battle to the finish, for the undismayed
preacher gathered himself together and ploughed on.
Dovebasket was looking pale and tense now. Was he
going to lose the day? Desperate measures must be taken.
He must play his last card. Trembling with excitement,
he leaned forward and pressed switch F under the pulpit.
Thank God, it worked. A six-pound boxing-glove slid
out of the wall with a smart click and dealt the reverend
gentleman a massive thump below the left ear. It was the
pay-off. He fell out of the crow's nest on to the much-
tried front rank of the Mission. His head came dreamily
to rest on Polk-Mowbray's knees. The world suddenly
looked brighter. I could hear the birds singing in the
Embassy shrubbery. Loving hands were there to gather
up the pieces, to dispose the body for burial. But Wilkinson still breathed. He was flown home on a stretcher at
Crown expense. Moreover, Drage was cured as if by a
miracle; at least temporarily. The cooking swung back
to good plain home. He still retained Wilkinson's Bible

and from time to time would read from it in a voice mossy with gutturals and general tonic sol fa. But the worst was over. Drage had become an ordinary butler again, a human being full of ordinary old-fashioned blood.

I could give you many other examples of what one might call the religious impulse in the Corps; it varied enormously. I hope Sam takes advantage of some of the more colourful episodes, like when Polk-Mowbray decided to build a Marxist chapel in the Embassy grounds to try and wean everyone from Barren Materialism. It got as far as the drawing-board stage before being shot down. Mercifully, political reasons intervened. For who would consecrate such a structure? The style was a sort of Primrose Hill Wesleyan. I believe John Betjeman was approached, but nothing came of it. The Russian Mission was particularly touchy. Their Chargé was a curious piece of Volga folklore called Damnovich. He had a sort of three-dimensional Marxist smile. He had been eaten into by the dialectic. One day he disappeared from sight and it was strongly rumoured that he had committed hara-kiri in the most original style. He had received a reproof for some minor dereliction of duty and took it so much to heart that he made the honourable amend by having himself marked TOP SECRET and carried out to the incinerator where he perished along with Confidential Waste. Clever, no? But not half as tortuous as Reggie Subtitle who was determined that his brother was not going to inherit a bean when he died. His will was a masterpiece. He had his embalmed body sent back to the sarcophagus in Coutts's Oxford Street Branch where it still lies in a cellar along with all his furniture and baggage. Nobody can get at it, and without it his brother

cannot inherit for Reggie is still posted as Missing—
Believed Absent, though all this is years ago now.

One last example—as a warning to junior dips. This
happened to me. You know that widowhood is practically a profession in Vulgaria; they were everywhere.
Widows. Dressed in rustling black, eyebrows meeting in
the middle, heavy moustaches. . . . Ninety per cent of the
population is widows, or so it seems. Well, we had one
of these, or rather, we acquired one. One of the Consular
Clerks had perhaps won her in a Christmas raffle? How
do I know? Took her instead of the turkey, or even by
mistake for it? At all events, she became Mrs Thread-
needle. Then her spouse tired of her, so he left his shoes
and clothes by the Danube, wrote her a curt farewell on
a leaf, and apparently drowned himself; in fact he panted
across the frontier and returned to civil life where he is
deeply respected in Banbury as an estate agent now. How
were we or she to know? We wrote him off and indented
for another. Meanwhile, Mrs Threadneedle, justifying
her existence, raised a Point of Order. Apparently widows
were no longer entitled to bonded drinks and smokes:
wives, yes. Not widows. She could not quite understand
this and her English was too sketchy to enable us to expose our case to her. It carried no conviction. Moreover,
she had somehow been led to believe that when one was
short of a British Subject, or when one had mislaid the
one in hand, one could simply trot up to the Mission and
select another. It was the question of bonded goods that
agitated her. She took to coming up and sitting outside
the Chancery door and pleading with us as we passed to
and fro. Finally she decided, since there was no help for
it, to select another spouse for herself so that the inter-
rupted flow of bonded gin and Benson and Hedges might

be resumed. Her choice fell upon me. I don't know why.
Perhaps it was my open face which seemed to betoken a
liberal nature. At any rate, when I passed her she would
point a finger at me and cry "I will 'ave 'im." It caused
a good deal of innocent amusement to all but myself. I
was scared stiff. Soon she made grabs at my hand to kiss.
The situation had become critical. I could only get to my
office now by climbing in at the window; moreover I
could only visit my colleagues in the same furtive way.
You can imagine how tiring this proved to be. My foot-
steps ploughed up the flower-beds. My muscles ached. I
lost weight. There seemed no way of getting rid of the
lady. Once she even came into my office with a priest
who blessed me with a sprig of hyssop and covered a
despatch with holy water. *She was paying to have me softened
up*. I was *in extremis*. Finally I consulted Dovebasket, and
it was thanks to his genius that the worst was averted.
Taking his advice, I called in Thurston and, clearing my
throat, put the matter to him. He was a huge fellow,
Chancery Guard.

"Thurston" I said, "you have rather a sharp choice
before you. You have been drunk on duty for the sixth
time running and H.E. has decided to tell the F.O. You
know what the result will be, don't you?"

He pulled a shaggy forelock and drew on the carpet
with his big toe. "Now" I went on, "he has left the whole
matter to my discretion. I have been pleading with him
on your behalf; but it seems to me that your whole
trouble is that you are a bachelor. You have too much
time on your hands and not enough responsibility. Now
if you married, I might reconsider the whole thing; moreover, if you married Mrs Threadneedle I might even upgrade and post you to somewhere where the pay is

better." I let all this sink in a bit. The fellow blenched, as well he might; but I pointed out that married men received splendid allowances and decent houses to live in. "Go away and debate the matter and let me have your reply not later than this evening." The firmness of my tone, the sweetness of my voice had a deep effect on him. By that evening he had made his choice: Mrs Thread-needle would become Mrs. Thurston. Imagine my relief. But the strange thing was that the marriage worked: Thurston signed the Pledge and started a new life. When I left, they were both singing in the choir. Say what you like, there must be something in religion.

The Little Affair in Paris

I wonder if I ever told you (said Antrobus) about the little affair in Paris? No? Well, normally I don't care to rake it up, it's too painful. But today I was reminded of it when I filled in my Insurance Medical. O'Toole swam into my mind's eye. My God, you have no idea.

The thing was I was going on leave and made the mistake of asking Polk-Mowbray if there was any little service I could perform for him in the capitals through which I was to pass. This, as you know, is the mere rhetoric of diplomacy; nobody but a swine would say yes there was. But he did. Fixing me with somewhat watery eyes he said in a dumb pleading tone: "You could be invaluable to me, Antrobus. Your mature judgement, your winning ways, your paternal touch. . . ." All this may have been true as far as it went. "I have a delinquent nephew called O'Toole" he went on "who is studying medicine in Paris. I fear that something terrible may befall him. He is baroque, quite baroque. His first report says that he is 'carrément funeste' whatever that is."

Mowbray's French is somewhat abraded like mine. I mean we can both say "Cueillez dès aujourd'hui les roses de la vie" with quite a good accent when passing through Customs, but though it creates atmosphere it is not much of a help.

I braced myself and pointed upwind. "Come, be a pal" he said. "All I ask is that you look him up and send me a Confidential Report on him. You may have much in common, who knows? After all, you'll be staying a day or so to cadge a free meal and rub noses with MacSalmon's Mission, won't you? Spare an afternoon for my wandering bairn."

Put this way it seemed cruel to refuse. I accepted—O woe to me, yes, I accepted. But the thing troubled me. As I rubbed on the mint-flavoured aftershave in the mirror of the Orient Express I looked at myself with affectionate misgivings. So beautiful and so Put-Upon.

All the omens were against me. I arrived in Paris during one of those long national holidays which can sometimes last a week. Nothing was open. No duty car. Even the Mission was locked up with everyone away. Even the Chargé was away hunting. The empty shell of the Embassy was in the charge of an illiterate washerwoman and a Chancery Guard smelling of absinthe. I had been counting on a sponge, food and lodging with some junior who would be proud to know me and house me. But more serious still was my lolly situation. I had hardly any real script on me and none of the crisp and crackling. I had drawn the usual vouchers for travel which would have enabled me to refill my tanks at selected points and leave not a wrack behind. Couldn't even change travellers' cheques supposing I had any. And here I was faced with the prospects of a hotel bill as well.

What to do? I pondered as I studied the news bulletin in the Chancery. There was not a name I knew on the Mission, not a friendly face. And my God, what low batting averages. I read down the list with sinking heart. Musgrave, Hoppner, Pratt, Brown . . . all names now famous to Interpol, but then unknown. They were all fledglings. It was a newly anointed Mission as far as I could see. Well, I walked round to try and raise the wind at Goupil, the Crillon, the Ritz and so on; nowhere could I find a hall porter I knew. Moreover my train did not leave till Monday. I would have to spend the week-end in Paris with nothing open but places of cultural repair like the Louvre—places where I might be exposed to an un-manning dose of unwanted culture. I knew how dangerous the French were. Anything but that. I walked about much struck by the many shops which stocked out-of-the-way literature and, if flush, might have bought a copy of *Unplanned Paternity*, being some hints to mothers by an Unplanned Father; which I believe was written by De Mandeville and Dovebasket under a pseudonym. But I daren't play fast and loose with my few francs. I had a glass of Prune Magic in a bistro and reflected on my lot. Finally I thought of O'Toole. Perhaps he might help? I unearthed his address. It was within walking distance of where I was. No harm, I thought, could come of passing that way, of conferring a timely nod, a cheerful word on O'Toole. I found the place quite easily, but it was fear-fully sinister, and there was a woman in a sort of box, who watched me carefully. She jumped when I men-tioned the name and produced a bloodstained cleaver from under her apron. She asked me to give him a message but I didn't manage to get its import. Yet it sounded men-acing. She punctuated with the cleaver. I raised my bowler and pressed on up the motheaten staircase to number thirteen. The bell being out of order I rapped with my gamp. There was a pause. Then suddenly everything happened as if in a film. The door flew open, something grabbed me by the necktie, dragged me within and shoved me up against a wall. The door shut behind me with a bang, and a knife was pressed into my tie. I was in the presence of O'Toole. "One word and I spit you" he hissed. I was far from uttering a word. I was stunned. He tugged me into a sort of studio and threw me on a couch where I rolled all over my bowler. "You have come from Them" he said "to spy on me. I told my uncle that the next one would suffer. And you're him." Ignoring his grammar I tried to adopt an ingratiating, a fragrant manner. It was no go. I was up against something beyond me. O'Toole looked like Dylan Thomas after a week on the tiles. Muffler and pork pie hat and all. He looked the hard core of Something. Clearly the soft answer would not suit. Moreover he smelt of plum brandy. He was beside himself. "Here I am beside myself with troubles and that manumitted mooncalf sends people to spy on me." His underlip trembled. Clearly the chap was hard pressed. I retrieved my bowler and cleared what was left of my throat. "Listen O'Toole" I said. "Calm your nerves and expose your case to me. Perhaps I can help." He gave a cry at this and advanced on me with knife raised. "Perhaps you can" he said. "Turn out your pockets." I'm afraid there was no abiding joy to be drawn from my wallet. Not content in spite of my honest look, he went through my pockets with a practised hand. No, this miserable sum was all I possessed. He walked up and down in a frenzy stabbing at the air. "What's the problem O'Toole?" I asked, and something feline and caressing in my tone must have touched a chord for he gave a strangled sob and said: "My rent is overdue and they are going to take Miriam away. They are distraining on me this evening." French bailiffs with heavy sideboards were on their way to do away with Polk-Mowbray's bairn. It was sad to see one so young so overwrought. "But they won't get her" he hissed. "I'd rather die." Gradually I brought myself to bear on the situation, to clarify it; some of what I tell you I only learned subsequently, of course. But for the nonce this reference to his paramour (it would take a Latin to distrain on a girl) nonplussed me. "Who and where is Miriam?" I asked looking round this gutted building. He pointed the tip of his awfully cutty knife— I can still show you the nick in my shirt where he pressed it home. The electric light had been cut off and the gloom was heavy; but in one corner of the room stood a sort of mummy case. He pointed wildly. "She's worth two hundred and fifty pounds" he said. "Moreover she is my aunt." Upon my word the damned thing was an articulated skeleton, the sort of thing medical men use to frighten each other on rag day. It was complete I mean down to the toe. It sagged from a hook in its neck; when you got closer it gave a queer sort of smile. I shuddered. But always loth to abandon a train of reasoning I asked O'Toole to exfoliate a bit, to expand, to explain. Well he had been brought up by a family of sawbones in Dublin who were devoted to the principles of the French Revolution. They had insisted that he study in Paris; Miriam his aunt had given her body to science for the honour of the family. It was their only heirloom. Apart from her they owned nothing. But magnanimously they gave it to him on his departure telling him, one supposes, to try and live up to it: and if not to flog it. Now it was going to be distrained upon. The more you see of life the less real it gets. . . . The fellow may have been a dastard but I could not help feeling a twinge of sympathy. He was feeling the draught. By skilful questioning I found out the rest. Apparently they could not distrain on him, only on his property; he had managed to get most of his clothes away by walking up and down the stairs in three or four suits at a time and stripping them off in the gents at the local bistro where his friend Coco kept an eye on them. "But if I tried to carry a bag down the concierge would be on me with that bloody cleaver. I shall have to leave my bags. But what about Miriam?" I could see no way round the affair. Then I saw his eyes narrow; he looked at me in rather a Pointed Way as if he were about to ask for a slice. "Why do you gaze on me like that?" I cried. I felt some ghastly notion coming over him. Nor was I wrong. "I have it" he cried waving his knife with renewed menace. "You say you've come to help me; well, so you shall." He opened the window and pointed into the street. "You will stand down there and I will lower Miriam to you" he said. "But if there is so much as a greenstick fracture on her when I get down your fate is sealed." I tried to remonstrate. After all, I pleaded, I was a British subject, a CMG, a Rotarian and a well-known handbells player. Surely he could not expect me to stand about on a Paris street corner with an unclothed aunt in my arms. He did. He poked me again. "And don't think you can leg it" he added. "I can throw this thing. Look!" He whirled round and pinked the kitchen cupboard.

Well it was a very subdued public servant that made his way down that creaking stair, tipping his bowler to the charmless dromedary in the box who still waited for the distraining force before launching an assault on number thirteen. It felt cold in the street. I felt a certain loss of reality coming over me; I mean it didn't seem to be me any more, my intrinsic me, waiting there gazing up to where, swaying slightly in the breeze, the bones of this venerable aunt descended towards me on a piece of stout cord. I took the pass all right. Miriam, rather heavier than you would expect, was safely in arms. "Now what?" I called anxiously up into the sky. A policeman had appeared down the corner of the street. He stopped dead in his tracks bemused by the spectacle. I felt deeply conscious of the unclothed nature of the specimen and shipped off my light green plastic mack to work on to her arms. The policeman watched this for a while, pale to the gills, and then muttering something about special tastes, turned round and ran back along the avenue blowing his whistle and calling for witnesses. This sort of thing could only happen at Lourdes, he must have said to himself. There was no time to explain and apologize for now O'Toole bounded from the door like a Michelin advertisement in his last three suits and four pullovers. "Run" he cried, and carried away by panic, I broke into a palsied gallop. We shared the burden of Miriam, bursting like a bomb into the bistro. "Saved" cried O'Toole. I don't know whether you have ever been around with a skeleton in a green plastic mack, old boy. I don't know how to describe the feeling. . . . It's uncanny. Most of the clients in the bistro paled under their tan, removed their pipes, seemed about to speak, and then just swallowed. O'Toole planked Miriam on a bar-stool and called for three tots. Coco, his friend, took the whole thing quite normally. I believe he thought that Miriam had been murdered by O'Toole and then put together in an idle

moment for the sake of company on wet Saturday evenings. I don't know. Anyway a long confab took place
about getting a decent price for her. This of course
caused ears to prick up and ribald comments to form on
various lips. Coco was for selling her to the Clinique des
Pieds Sensibles, but once more we were stymied by this
public holiday. It was shut. I was so worked up now that
I drank Miriam's glass off. Along the street there was
trouble starting; fortunately the police had thrown a net
around this house whose inhabitants spent their time
cutting up aunts only to fall upon the distraining party,
bailiffs and beadles and whatnot dressed in opera hats and
cloaks. Thank God we were just clear; the police arrested
the distrainers who resisted arrest violently. Watching
them I felt no joy; only misgiving. For there on the stool,
smiling slightly, sat this damned skeleton. We lay low for
hours while Coco gave us drinks and marked them on
a score card. He told us about his political life. He
turned out to be a red hot revolutionary who walked
about Paris at night chalking "Coco est traitre" and
"Français à moi" on the walls. His party had a resounding
name but according to O'Toole only one member, himself. Eclectic stuff. But time was getting on; I had to take
myself off and said so. "By God you are going to stay
with me to the end" cried O'Toole, "or by the bones of
Polk-Mowbray I'll slit your F.O. weasand." Polk-Mowbray! I thought of him with such distaste at that moment.
Here I was penniless and trapped by this aunt-fixated and
fuliginous fool.

Coco tried to cheer us up with a song—and he had a
fine set of pipes—but I was in no mood for joy. O'Toole
thought deeply. Then he said he had it. There was one
person who would pay him a decent price for Miriam, a

chap called Raoul. But Raoul lived some way outside Paris. We would have to borrow some money somehow. He would pawn a couple of suits with Coco for the journey. "I don't want to go on any journey" I wailed. "Silence Anchovy" he thundered. "We are in this thing to the death now." It was what I very much feared; but I felt weak and defenceless. Miriam had sort of moulded me to her bony will. I won't describe our stately progress across Paris—I'm saving it for the second volume of my memoirs. O'Toole was now under the influence and disposed to be lighthearted to the point of coarseness. But have you ever turned round in a bus-queue and seen a skeleton in a plastic mack at your elbow? We spread dismay wherever we went. On the top of a bus he sat Miriam in the seats reserved for the Mutilés de La Guerre and refused to buy a ticket, saying that Miriam had fallen on the Marne. The ticket-collector's face worked, his moustache swivelled through 365 degrees but what could he say? How could he prove anything? Several times we lost our way. Once I had to stand alone holding Miriam while O'Toole visited one of those tin shelters where you can see the customers' legs underneath. I was standing on the steps of St Sulpice when another policeman came up to make conversation; did he fear a riot? Did he suspect a crime? I shall never know. He tried to address me, very civilly I mean, and pointed at Miriam. "C'est la plume de ma tante" I tried to explain, "Mademoiselle Miriam." He said "Tiens" and raised his shako. But I was so overcome by this effort to explain, and by O'Toole's prolonged absence, that I rushed into the church and hid in a side-chapel. I had hardly started the Lord's Prayer with Miriam kneeling beside me when a verger, white to the lips, came up and hissed at me. "Get that thing out of here, you are frightening the customers" was clearly the import of his remarks. Foiled in my intercession with the All-Highest I retreated to the steps and once more met up with O'Toole. Another bus-ride followed, and yet another. I began to feel that everyone in the city must now have seen us with our strange companion. Some thought we were advertising orthopaedic devices. Others that we were Burke and Hare, grave-robbers on a spree. The most charitable felt that we were enjoying a rather unhealthy drollery on our way to the boneyard.

From time to time I half awoke from my tranced state and prayed aloud. But Miriam only smiled. Never have I felt so much the centre of attention. But worse was to follow. We arrived deep in the countryside at a place which sounded like St Abdomen La Boue. We dragged Miriam across a churchyard watched by the furtive peasantry huddled behind trees and in copses. We sounded a bell, a door opened and there was Raoul, beret on head and pipe in mouth; we thought we were safe especially as he was overjoyed to see Miriam and agreed on the spot to find her a good home. In fact he waltzed round the room with her in a paroxysm of delight. Then he stopped and his face clouded. Apparently he also was in some kind of trouble. He had fallen foul of the local parson and been denounced from the St Abdomen pulpit on suspicion of practising black magic; the thing was he was trying to grow salads in his garden by the Rudolf Steiner bio-organic method. I am not clear about it but I gathered that in order to get the things to push one had to catch them at full moon, and walk round them reciting mystic runes and playing on a pipe. Enough to cause the darkest suspicions I'll allow. In fact things had become so hot that he was thinking of shutting up the house and returning to

Paris. While he was explaining all this the phone rang. He answered it and jumped a foot in the air. "They are on their way to arrest me. Someone has told the police that they saw people dragging bodies out of the graveyard next door and bringing them in here. There is no time to lose." I clutched my umbrella until my knuckles turned white. What new horrors lay in store for us? Outside a sullen church bell began to beat; one could hear the muttering crowd; some stones pelted against the front gate. We sat staring at each other unnerved. Then afar off across the countryside one heard the yapping of a police car racing towards us. "Quick" cried Raoul. "We must escape." Once again I was seized with vertigo. I cannot remember clearly what happened—how we found ourselves in Raoul's little car, all of us. I sat in the back with Miriam on my knee. As we roared out of the gate in a rain of clods a demoniac scream went up from a thousand throats. Their worst suspicions had been confirmed. A scream of pure horror. Surely a bit exaggerated, but then the untutored peasantry are like that. After all, I was still quite tidily dressed and wearing my bowler. There was no need to imagine that. . . .

Across country we went like the wind followed by a couple of black cars full of moustaches. They were gaining on us. "Faster" cried O'Toole, and Raoul pressed down until the thing was level with the floorboards. We were cornering much too fast to judge by the scraping noise. Nor could this speed be maintained. We came round a corner and were confronted by a locked level crossing. It was too late to brake. Raoul made a majestic attempt to leap the obstacle; we careered off to one side, through a field and then went smack into the heart of a haystack. I think I must have lost consciousness; all was smoke, darkness and tickle. But when at last I was disinterred I felt a great sense of relief for Miriam was no more. She had been dashed into a thousand fragments. So indeed had we all. The gallant constabulary disinterred us, placed us on ladders and took us back to the ambulance. The next thing was I woke up in the next bed to O'Toole in the local hospital at Moisson. I ached all over but nothing was broken. My nose was blue—this part here. It was a relatively lucky escape. As I lay in a half trance I heard two medical men arguing about our case and the treatment thereof. O'Toole was shamming dead but listening carefully. One voice said "I disagree with you Armand. The Cordon Rouge is powerful enough in a case like this." The other voice shook its head and said: "In my opinion only the Imperial will answer." A frail tremor of joy fluttered in my breast. I blessed a medical profession enlightened enough to prescribe vintage champagne in such cases; it is good for shock, good for bruises, good for everything. Moreover Imperial Tokay, Mumm's Cordon Rouge . . . I didn't really care which. The voices died away and we were alone again. I chuckled and leaned over to O'Toole. "Did you hear that?" I said. "We are going to get a champers treatment. Isn't it bully?" But he was bright green, his lips moved in prayer. "Anchovy" he said at last, "you know not what you are saying. Your blithe innocence cuts me to the heart. *The Imperial and the Cordon Rouge are the largest suppositories known to science.*" My God! I had forgotten the obsession of the French medical man with the homely suppos. It is prescribed for everything from coated tongue to tertiary gangrene. I don't wish to argue its merits or demerits as a treatment. I have no doubt that in many a difficult case it works. *But it is prescribed for everything.* There is no way round it.

There I was at the mercy of men with these weird pro-
clivities. How would I ever face The Office again? A
cry burst from my lips. "Never!" I meant it. I was seized
by a sort of frenzy. In a moment I had stripped off my
bandages, and vaulted out of my nightshirt into my
trousers. Bowler and umbrella were on the end of the
bed. "Goodbye O'Toole" I cried in the voice of a lion
and with one bound was at the door. I passed the nurse on
the stairs. She was carrying a sort of bazooka on a tray. I
think she only caught sight of a flash of white as I streaked
past her out into the surrounding countryside. The emergency brought out all that was most resourceful in
Antrobus. I thumbed a ride on a van into Paris and made
my way back to the Embassy determined to sleep on the
doorstep if necessary. But by a stroke of good luck
Glamis Tadpole had come back and was now receiving.
All my troubles were at an end. I accepted a glass of
Scotch and relaxed in the armchair while he made pleasant
conversation. "I must say" he said "you look very relaxed.
You must have had a jolly week-end."

Little did he know. Sometimes in my dreams Miriam
returns to visit me; but she has begun to fade. Only
now I have got into the habit of by-passing Paris on my
journeys. A man of my age and in my position of trust
can't be too careful, can he?

Taking the Consequences

I have never (said Antrobus) ceased to preach against paper games in the leisure hours of the service; either for entertainment of friends or for the killing of time. I have several times found them a Grave Danger. Nor do I make any exception—though perhaps the game called "Consequences" is the worst in this respect. To my regret Polk-Mowbray could never be got round to this view; for him no dinner party was complete without a vapid hand of Pontoon, or Mimsy or Bellweather. All the pencils were co-opted from Chancery, and all the expensive minute-paper. Down we would sit to wrestle with some inane problem, feeling like a human fritter; nor could we say him nay. He *ordered* us to play. It was inhuman, and at times I got so indignant that I thought I should get circles under my prose or lose my *vibrato* or both. But Nemesis was waiting in the podgy person of the Baron Blenkinhoorn, the newly arrived correspondent of the Deutsches Sauerkraut news agency, a powerful organ of West German opinion. He was a very serious man. His notepaper had a crown and garter gules. He wore heavy spectacles and beard brushed back against the wind like Epping Forest. Whatever you told him he wrote down instantly in a huge pad and telegraphed to his organ. He lived in the Vulgaria Hotel and was rumoured to sleep with a pistol under his pillow. Nor did his seriousness make him endearing, no. Once De Mandeville persuaded him to publish Polk-Mowbray's obituary by uttering a false press release. For a man as superstitious as our Ambassador this gave him quite a fright and the Baron had some trouble exculpating himself. Quite a huff grew up between them and it was only rarely that the Baron came into the Chancery for a brief untainted bit of info. On some such visit he must have managed to break down the morale of Dovebasket and make a hireling of him, for his despatches were now full of Inside Info, things he would never have known had he not had an accomplice. For instance that Toby Imhof was even then working on bottled cat's breath to put down mouseholes and had already patented the perfected version of Snarlex, jujube for the tired parent. Where could he have found out I mean? Even the little day-to-day accidents which any normal Embassy has to endure without telling the press. The Baron knew them all and sent them to his organ which duly printed. Nothing appeared to be sacred. It was the year that Angela was sent down for writing Just Married on the back of a police car; Dovebasket, who was mad about her and had been jilted revenged himself by meddling with the taps on the blue room bidet—to such good effect that the wretched girl found herself pinned to the ceiling by a water-jet and had to be got down with ladders. You see what I mean? He finally had us looking over our shoulders. Polk-Mowbray bit his

nails to the quick. Particularly as all this stuff was joyfully translated by our German Mission and sent back to
the F.O. The Foreign Secretary read with popping eye
the Baron's account of De Mandeville's dress reform
movement which insisted on handbags for men and the
wearing of a strange new hat called a Boadicea, with side
flaps. The wires began to buzz and we found ourselves
issuing Categorical Denials or Studied Evasions in batches
of ten. Things could not go on like this. But how to get
the Baron out? If only we could get him declared persona
non grata by the Vulgarians. . . . But his integrity was
perfect, he neither smoked nor drank, and women were
mere furniture. We ran through a number of schemes,
mostly counsels of desperation, like introducing highly
trained crabs into his bath. De Mandeville who was white
with rage tried to get up a plot to murder him outright by
waxing the dance floor to a preternaturally high gloss
and inviting the Baron to a ball where Angela, who had
agreed to sacrifice herself, was to lead him out for a
Waltz and then turn him loose to break his neck. We were
foiled. The Baron didn't dance, and of those who did
several broke their collar bones and ankles. No, he was a
tough nut to crack. We put Scooter our secret service
fellow on to him, to study his little weaknesses; but he
had few, unless you count spending hours and hours
alone playing on a portable clavicord.

Meanwhile the Revelations went on; some of them were
so extraordinary that Polk-Mowbray nearly went out of
his mind. The Foreign Sec. wrote him in prose of a
secular tautness, asking him whether or not the following
were true: a secret meeting with Mrs Krushchev to
negotiate a pact without telling H.M.G. Another less
secret with Pandit Nehru outside a public *cabinet d'aisance*

in Bombay. A third with Stalin. A fourth with the Baroness of Monrovia (a dusky Ambassadress) . . . And so on. "Antrobus" he cried out, "somehow this must stop. Simple denials cannot meet the case. Everyone believes the press, nobody believes a dip. This man has set out to lose me my froggings. Think, man, think." I thought until I throbbed. Then the idea crept over me that recently we had not heard very much of Dovebasket; he had been living a life of strange and rather suspicious demureness. Something Told Me that if he were not directly responsible for those leaks he might at least have a notion about what to do. I went to see him and tried to rouse his manlier feelings by describing the emotions of Polk-Mowbray. He only laughed like a faun and said "So he has had enough has he? I was wondering when he would break. Yes, I know what to do, but it will take money and time. For a couple of hundred I could suborn Blenkinhoorn." The price was outrageous of course but we were trapped. "So you *are* responsible after all" I blazed at him, white to the tentacles and practically springing a front stud. "Explain yourself."

He wouldn't until I'd handed over the money. Dovebasket counted it respectfully and stowed. Then he said: "Actually old Blenky is acting in perfect good faith; it's just that he is short on humour and doesn't know how the other half live. His vision is warped. I was just about to send him over another lot of info for tomorrow's organ. But since you ask so nicely I'll desist. Here, have a look. There's no mystery; I've been selling him the fruit of H.E.'s wastepaper basket. He will insist on paper games."

I saw a clutch of paper Consequences which explained all. The Baron had been working upon texts which must

have seemed mysterious enough to him in all consequence
but which were as clear as daylight to the normal F.O.
mind:

> *The British Ambassador met*
> *Mrs Krushchev*
> *In a lift*
> *He said: "Will you be my satellite?"*
> *She said "Squeeze me when the lights go out."*
> *The result was The Warsaw Pact*
> *Polk-Mowbray met*
> *Pandit Nehru*
> *Outside a public lavatory in Bombay*
> *He said: "Never a dull moment"*
> *N replied: "I would sell you my soul"*
> *The result was a small inedible. . . .*

But why go on? In a flash one could see how the Baron
had been misled. I mounted triumphantly to Mowbray
and waved the papers. I told him how I had saved the
day. The money would have to come from the secret
fund of course. He mopped his brow and thanked me
fervently. Yet Dovebasket did not escape a Grave Reproof. I distinctly heard Polk-Mowbray saying to him on
the phone: "You can damn well take a hundred lines,
Dovebasket, yes a hundred. And let them be 'In future I
must not be such a blasted Borrogrove.' "

I thought that rather met the case.

All to Scale

The thing was (said Antrobus) that Professor Regulus was sent to us by Protocol as the Embassy sawbones. He was a nice compact little man with *pince-nez* and a fine reputation with the full syringe. Moreover he was pro-British, unhealthily so as it turned out. He kept closely in touch with home affairs, borrowed my *Times* and so on; and this was how he got to learn of the PM's gout. I expect you remember the time when it got so bad there was talk of a Day of National Temperance and Prayer, a special service in Paul's and so on. Well Regulus took it much to heart and one Monday he tapered up to the Mission holding a bottle of something called The Regulus Tincture—his own invention he said. He set it down on my desk and gave me a brief insight into gout. It was, he said, just a sort of scale which collected on the big toe like the scale in a kettle. His Tincture, which was made of a mixture of arrowroot and henbane on a molasses base and macerated with borage—his Tincture simply dissolved the scale and liberated the shank. It had, I must say, a funny sort of colour; when you shook the bottle it kind of seethed. I took it in to show Polk-Mowbray who was very touched by this proof of anglophile concern. "By Gad" he said, "we shall pack it off to the PM. Perhaps there's enough for the whole front bench. What a fine fellow Regulus is. Stap me but I'll put him up for a gong." I went down to have the bottle wrapped up and bagged; on the way I met Dovebasket, who was always keen on science, and dazzled him a little with my grasp of things medical. "Just like scale?" he said with curiosity. "I think we ought to try a drop or two." I did not quite understand, but followed him into the garden where his new sports car stood. Before I could bring to bear he had tipped a cupful of the Tincture into the radiator. Talk about scale! There was a tinkle and a rain of scale fell out on the gravel. Smoke rose from the radiator tap. "Stand back" I cried. It was heating up. There was a snap. . . . By Goodness this was some mixture. "We ought to try some on Drage" he said moodily, but I did not want to experiment any further. The stuff was good on scale and that's as far as I wanted to go. I didn't wish to probe any further. I hoped it would bring great and lasting benefit to the nation and the party. I took the bottle down to bag room and sped it off.

Some time passed before we heard anything from London; then came a somewhat sullen response saying that the PM had tried it on one of his foodtasters who had gone berserk and run the length of Ealing Broadway shouting "Thrope for Labour"—his name. The bottle was returned to us with this disquieting information and with the distinct order from the F.O. to try it out in the Mission and to report on its properties to the Foreign Secretary. Well, I mean to say: I have never been backward when it comes to self-sacrifice but I did not fancy a dessert-spoonful of this stuff after what I had seen it do to Dovebasket's radiator. Besides the only one of us who was honestly scaly was Polk-Mowbray; he had in fact been rather proud of his gout and inclined to boast about it. Here was his chance, you would have said; but no he did not seem to see it in this light. He sat, a somewhat pale individual in his heather mixture, and glared at the bottle on his desk. "I don't want to be cured of my gout" he wailed. "It's the one proof I have that the blood of the fourteenth earl runs, though in somewhat tributary fashion, through my veins."

We debated the whole matter at length; the F.S.'s order could not be lightly set aside. Someone would have to report. Finally it was decided to try a control experiment on Drage and see how that went. It was not hard, for Drage used to drink an occasional glass of Gaskin's Imperial Ginger Wine; in fact he was allowed whenever we had a Royal Toast with lowered lights etc. to join us in pledging his sovereign with a sip of the cordial muck. What easier than to insert a normal dose of the Tincture into his bottle? We watched with intense scientific curiosity that night as Polk-Mowbray dowsed the glims and raised his glass while Drage padded across the room to his cordial and poured out a medium-sized firkin of the stuff.

It was impressive, even riveting. The fellow appeared to have swigged off a glass full of molten lead. A high screech rang out, and he seized his own ears as if he were about to pull them off. Then he started to shadow box, upsetting the candles, and incidentally setting himself alight. What with trying to restrain and comfort him and at the same time to beat out his burning waistcoat there was a vast amount of confusion. What an impartial observer would have made of the scene I know not. Drage vaulted on to the window-sill and still screeching raced off into the night like a hare, tearing off burning articles of clothing as he ran. He left us, a sobered group of palish persons contemplating the ruins of the dinner and the fearful effects of the Regulus syndrome. "By God, what cracking stuff" said Polk-Mowbray. "I suppose we'd better tell the police to look out for a flaming butler what?" It was a pity really that the PM hadn't had the benefits of this terrific tonic; he might have galvanized the party on it. But our hearts were heavy, for we loved Drage; and there he was galloping across Vulgaria tracing a comet's path. It was three days before the police found him and brought him back to us on a stretcher looking pale but sentient. He told us that the stuff had *turned him into a werewolf* for twenty-four hours. At this Polk-Mowbray, always capricious, suddenly flew into a temper with Regulus. "Imagine it" he cried, "this man solemnly urging on us stuff capable of turning a Head of Mission into a werewolf, however harmless. By Gad it is not in nature. It might have happened to me anywhere. Suppose I had bitten Hasdrubal or some other member of the Central Committee? I must speak to Regulus and sharply."

But the next morning the O.B.E. which Polk-Mowbray had secured for Regulus came through on the wire. "It's a bitter pill to swallow" he said. "Just as I was about to berate the man here comes this blasted decoration; what possessed me to do it?" How was I to know what possessed him? One could only say that at the best of times Polk-Mowbray's sense of cause and effect was jolly sketchy. "And the final annoyance" he said, giving rein to his mean side "is that we'll have to toast him in champagne and it's gone up a pound a case." By custom Heads of Mission paid for this out of their own *frais*. It was Dovebasket who suggested that we should touch up the Professor's drinks with the Tincture as a sort of revenge, and on the purely superficial plane the idea had charm. But the risks were great. We could not have werewolves cantering about the Embassy grounds yelling "Thrope for Labour" in Vulgarian and perhaps dishing out septic bites. No. We debated the matter from every angle but finally we agreed that Regulus should drink of the true the blushful in a state of nature: if there were any beaded bubbles winking at the brim it wouldn't be the Tincture. So grave was the danger, however, that I did not dare to leave the bottle lying about. Not with people like Dovebasket and De Mandeville in the Mission. So we trotted solemnly out on the lawn in the presence of each other and there I uncorked and poured away the Tincture. Everything smoked and turned blue for a minute. Then we walked back through the clouds to the buttery for a Bovril. If ever you revisit the Vulgarian Mission you will see that there is a huge circle burnt in the lawn; despite every effort nothing has ever managed to grow in that place. Some Tincture, what?

Aunt Norah

More than once (said Antrobus) have I seen my Chief shaken, sometimes even brought close to breaking point: but you should have seen his face when intelligence came that his Aunt Norah was heading south towards Vulgaria, leaving a train of carnage behind her in Paris and Rome. It was a cruel thing to happen to him, particularly at his time of life with retirement so near. Yes, he was old by then, a somewhat battered repaint; but this bit of news had him skipping like a stag. In those days he was rumoured to wear dunlopillo trousers so that he could sit down without bruising his ideas—but this was mere malice on the part of Dovebasket. Aunt Norah now. . . . Of a sudden he was sad, bowed; he lowered his under-carriage and trimmed his flaps and cried: "No." Once, just like that, "No."

I cannot disguise the fact from you that she had gone a little queer in the head with the passage of the years. At first she was mildly eccentric; but what got her turned off clear was that she happened upon some Labour Party pamphlets and was at once captivated by their attitude to sex. I mean about having lots more about and teaching the young and so on; and to have more pictures of Bernard Shaw over the nuptial bed to promote conception. I don't know. I never took a lot of it in myself. Rum stuff I found it, in places downright unmannerly. But that is what Labour stands for they say. Well anyway the Scales Fell from Aunt Norah's eyes when she read Shaw on how to be more all-embracing. Why Shaw I wonder? Nobody came down with powder markings after kissing him did they? Anyway she was converted and decided to promote the good cause by lecturing on sex to the young of foreign nations, starting with the French. Of course the trouble is that you can't illustrate sex for young people as clearly as you can Euclid; the human body has too few acute angles or hypotenuses—or so they tell me. But she did her best. Her huge diagrams looked like a study of the internal measurements of the Grand Pyramid; there were logarithms, isotherms, isobars and heavy pressure belts like a weather forecast. It was impressive. We first heard of traffic jams and cheering crowds and police charges in Paris. The French love intellectual diversions and here she was; she lectured from a table covered in a Union Jack and with a bull terrier called Bernard tied to the leg. She had trained it to growl at various points in her lecture as if to give point to it. Of course all this may have seemed a bit strange to them but then everyone knows that the British have their own way of doing things.

So now Aunt Norah was heading south after tearing Rome apart. "If storied urn or animated bust" I reflected as I saw my Chief sitting there with bowed head looking as if he had been passed through muslin and was weak and fizzy enough to be sipped through a straw. "I will

hand over the administration of the secret fund for
ONE WHOLE WEEK to whoever can think of a way to stop
her" he vowed. Naturally such an idea had great appeal
and many were the ideas tried out. De Mandeville, pushed
for lolly as always, hit upon a notion that almost worked;
he and his chauffeur dressed up as Carmelites and delivered
an aide-mémoire to the Vulgarian F.O. protesting about
her being allowed in on religious grounds. They were
somewhat shaken but stood firm. I think they had glimp-
sed the suede hacking-shoes underneath the gown. Or
perhaps their rosaries looked dubious. Anyway Polk-
Mowbray's alarm communicated itself to all of us; we
grew morose, edgy, jumpy. After prayers one day De
Mandeville struck his head on a beam and was knocked
almost insensible; we had to give him the kiss of life with
a bicycle pump. When he came to he confessed that he
thought he saw Aunt Norah advancing down the drive,
hence the jump. Just to show you what a state we were in.

Meanwhile the lady herself was advancing methodically
on the capital in a large caravan with "Hurrah For Sex"
on one side, "Glory to the population bulge" on the
other; she pursued her leisurely course across the smiling
countryside, stopping in the little towns to dish out
pamphlets and fertility charms and harangue the multi-
tudes. Of course they couldn't understand . . . and this
is where Dovebasket earned a whole week of the secret
fund. His face ablaze with joy he rushed into the Chancery
shouting: "I've got it." We hardly dared to hope by this
time. "We are fools" said the youth. "Aunt Norah
knows not a word of Vulgarian, and who in Vulgaria
knows more than the words 'whisky and soda' in our
native bow-wow?" We mulled him over a bit. "But the
riots in Paris and Rome, the march on Florence—how

was this achieved, for clearly she knows neither French nor Italian?" Dovebasket whinnied. "Of course. *Interpreters*. We must offer her official interpreters and then suborn them. While she thinks she is throwing them into a fine lather with her sex palaver they can be reading strips of Holy Writ like Engels or Kingsley Martin. In this way we will save our souls." Polk-Mowbray had tears in his eyes. "I believe you have it, my boy" he said fishing out the key and handing it over. "Now we must find the translators. Yea, go out Antrobus and find me two little Vulgarians with flared nostrils and ears too close to the head—men with the bad breath of taxmen or Marxists." For once I saw the road clear. "Ay Ay, sir" I said; and so the whole matter fell out. Aunt Norah had one of the most successful rallies of her tour and apart from us all being deafened by Engels all was well.

9

A Corking Evening

All day today (said Antrobus) I have been addressing Christmas Cards, an occupation both melancholy and exhilarating; so many of us have gone leaving no address. They have become "F.O. BAG ROOM PLEASE FORWARD" so to speak. Some are Far Flung, some less Far Flung, some Flung out altogether like poor Toby. It is a season which sets one wondering where dips go when they die, old man. Do they know that they can't take it with them, or is there perhaps a branch of Coutts' in Heaven which will take post-dated cheques? And if they live on as ghosts, what sort of? Is there a diplomatic Limbo— perhaps some subfusc department of UNO where they are condemned perpetually to brood over such recondite subjects as the fishing rights of little tufted Papuans? Ah me! But perhaps it would be more like some twilit registry where a man might yet sit down to a game of coon-can with a personable cipherine. . . .

Yes, as I riffled my address book so many forgotten faces drifted across my vision! Who will ever tell their story? Not me. What has become of Monksilver and Blackdimple—those two scheming Jesuits? What of "Tumbril" Goddard who believed in the Soviet way of life until he tried *kvass*? What of old "Tourniquet" Mathews, and "Smegma" Schmidt, the Polish avalanche? If ever the secret history of The Office is written their names will be blazoned abroad. Some have never had their due—like poor little Reggie and Mercy Mucus, the British Council couple. They died in the execution of their duty, eaten by wolves. Despite a falling glass they tried to cross the frozen lake bearing a sackful of Collins' Clear Type Shakespeares; they were heading for some remote and fly-blown khan where their eager clientele of swineherds waited patiently, eager to ingest all this foreign lore. In vain! In vain!

Then my eye fell upon the name of Dovebasket and forgotten scenes thronged back, one more painful than the next. I remembered, for example, the age of emulation ... I have often remarked how emulous Heads of Mission can be. That winter it was champagne. Several old European cellars had been up for sale, and those who had not overspent on their *frais* had cried Snap, among them Polk-Mowbray. He was at that time going through a difficult period. He had become much enamoured of young Sabina Braganza, daughter of an Italian colleague; mind you, all this in a perfectly proper and avuncular way. When she announced her engagement, he was so pleased that he decided to throw a party for the event which would both celebrate her beauty and allow him to show off his champagne. Though often misguided, he was a good man at heart. But he had offended Dovebasket. And Dovebasket harboured a Grave Grudge. He decided to touch up, or as he put it to "excite", Polk-Mowbray's cherished cases of Pommery. With a blowlamp in hand and clad in a steel-welder's casque he prowled the cellars like a figure from Greek tragedy, warming the stuff up and loosening the wire. The result was unforeseen but satisfying from his point of view. The banqueting room was shaken by dull explosions; some of the bottles went off like Mills bombs, others threw out parabolas of foam. I saw Drage holding one of these spouting bottles up with the astonished look of a man whose umbrella has been blown inside out. Worst of all the Braganza child received a black eye from a cork.

The failure of this party and the fury of the parents all but unhinged Polk-Mowbray; he took to locking himself up, talking to himself, even to starving a bit. It got to such a pitch that he even started sleepwalking. One morning Drage saw him in the dim light of dawn walking out of the Embassy and into the road clad in the blue night-shirt he always wore (with royal arms embroidered on it). It was horrifying. There was our Head of Mission crossing the main road in his tasselled bed-cap, hands outstretched, lips moving. Drage sped after him, Bible in hand. He tried to wake him by talking to him, but in vain. He dared not actually shake him for the person of a Plenipotentiary Extraordinary is sacred and can only be touched, pushed or pulled by someone of equal rank. Drage was at his wits' end; he even read bits of the Gospel loudly to his chief, but to no purpose. All he heard was the muttered whisper "I have come to apologize."

They were nearly run down by an early-morning tram full of workmen who cheered them. Then, with increased horror Drage saw him turn into the gate of the Italian Mission and start climbing the ivy towards the second floor where the unfortunate Braganza girl slept. Drage held one ankle and yelled for help. Now the situation was only saved by an extraordinary coincidence. De Mandeville had been on a diet that week, and had been limiting himself to a glass of early morning dew which he gathered himself from the Embassy grass. It was he who, glass in hand, heard Drage's yell from across the road. He bounded to the rescue, and less intimidated by Polk-Mowbray's rank than the butler, sacrificed the dew he had gathered by pouring it down his Ambassador's back.

Polk-Mowbray awoke with a start and fell, bringing down most of the trellis with him. There was a moment of Agonizing Reappraisal as the three of them sprawled among the flowerbeds. Then Polk-Mowbray realized where he was though he wotted not quite how. They rushed, they ran, they galloped back to the safety of the Mission. That morning Drage served them an early breakfast in the buttery and Polk-Mowbray swore De Mandeville to secrecy; he also told him that he was putting him up for the Life Saving Medal—a cherished decoration normally only given to people who rescue dogs from wells. "Furthermore" he added—for he knew how to do the handsome thing—"I want to apologize for making you waste your dew. I know it is jolly hard work gathering it."

"Not at all, Sir, there is plenty more where it came from." Upon which amiable exchange the incident was closed. Another sherry?